# Ceremonies and Celebrations
# BIRTHS

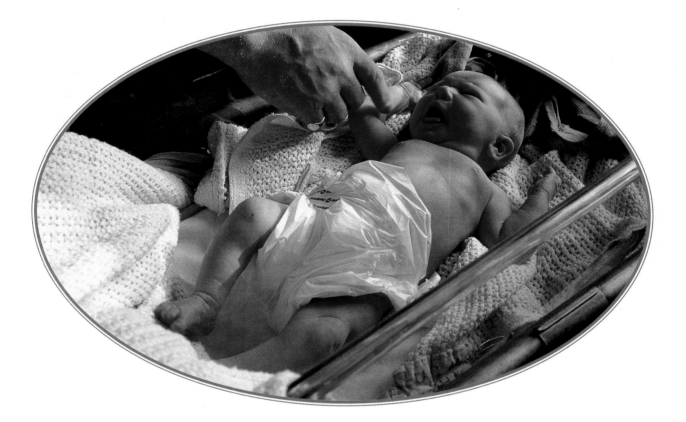

## JACQUELINE DINEEN

RAINTREE
STECK-VAUGHN
RSVP PUBLISHERS

A Harcourt Company

Austin   New York
www.steck-vaughn.com

## Ceremonies and Celebrations
# BIRTHS

## Other titles in this series are:
# WEDDINGS • FEASTS AND FASTING • GROWING UP • LIFE'S END • PILGRIMAGES AND JOURNEYS

**Consultants:**

**Khadijah Knight** is a teacher and consultant on multicultural education and Islam. She is also the author of several children's books about Islam.

**Marcus Braybrooke** is a parish priest and lecturer and writer on inter-faith relations. He is joint President of the World Congress of Faiths.

**Kanwaljit Kaur-Singh** is a local authority inspector for education. She has written many books on the Sikh tradition and appears on television regularly.

**Sharon Barron** regularly visits schools to talk to children about Judaism. She has written two books about Judaism.

**Meg St. Pierre** is the Director of the Clear Vision Trust, a charitable trust that aims to inform and educate about the teachings of Buddha.

**V.P. Hemant Kanitkar** is a retired teacher and author of many books on Hinduism.

© Copyright 2001, text, Steck-Vaughn Company

Published by Raintree Steck-Vaughn Publishers,
an imprint of Steck-Vaughn Company

Printed in Italy. Bound in the United States.
1 2 3 4 5 6 7 8 9 0 05 04 03 02 01

Library of Congress Cataloging-in-Publication Data

Dineen, Jacqueline.
    Births / Jacqueline Dineen.
        p.    cm.—(Ceremonies and celebrations)
    Includes bibliographical references and index.
    ISBN 0-7398-3267-0
    1. Religions—Juvenile literature.
    [1. Religions.]
    I. Title.  II. Series.

**Picture acknowledgments**

Circa Picture Library 15 (John Smith), 16, 18, 22, 28, 29; Hutchinson Library 4 (Juliet Highet), 9 (N. Durrell McKenna), 24 (Liba Taylor); Panos Pictures 6 (Betty Press), 8 (Jon Spaull), 17 (Giacomo Airozzi), 19 (Chris Stowers), 21 (Jean-Leo Dugast), 27 (Jimmy Holmes); Peter Sanders 14; Robert Harding Picture Library *front cover* top left (N. Hall/Shout); Tony Stone Images *title page*, 5; Trip *front cover* top right (I. Genut), bottom left (Resource Foto), bottom right (H. Rogers), 7 (A. Tovy), 10 (I. Genut), 11 (I. Brahim), 12 (I. Genut), 13 (I. Genut), 20 (H. Rogers), 23 (F. Good), 25 (F. Good), 26 (B. Dhanjal).

# CONTENTS

# Preparing for Parenthood

Just about everywhere in the world, the birth of a new baby is a very special time. Many couples go into marriage hoping and praying for a baby. Sometimes the parents have prepared for months and waited anxiously for the baby's arrival. They realize that they are bringing a new individual into the world and that this is a great responsibility.

People worship in many different ways throughout the world, and most societies have their own way of welcoming a new baby. In most cultures, as they wait for their new baby, a couple considers how they will bring the child up to be a good person. Often they will look to their religion to give them guidance in their child's upbringing.

*As the day of the birth approaches, many couples try to decide what to call their new child. Many babies are named after older family members to give the child a sense of belonging.* ▶

As the time for the birth approaches, the parents-to-be may worry about whether their baby will be healthy. When the baby is born safely, it is a time for celebration and thanksgiving. For people who follow a religious faith, one of the main ways to give thanks is to hold a religious celebration.

▼ As soon as a baby is born, whether it is in a hospital or at home, family members visit the mother and her new baby to wish them good luck and happiness.

# Preparing the room

The parents prepare for the birth in practical ways. They buy things for the baby and prepare a room for it to sleep in. Often the families of the couple expecting the child give them gifts of baby clothes and toys to welcome the new baby into the family and to help the parents financially.

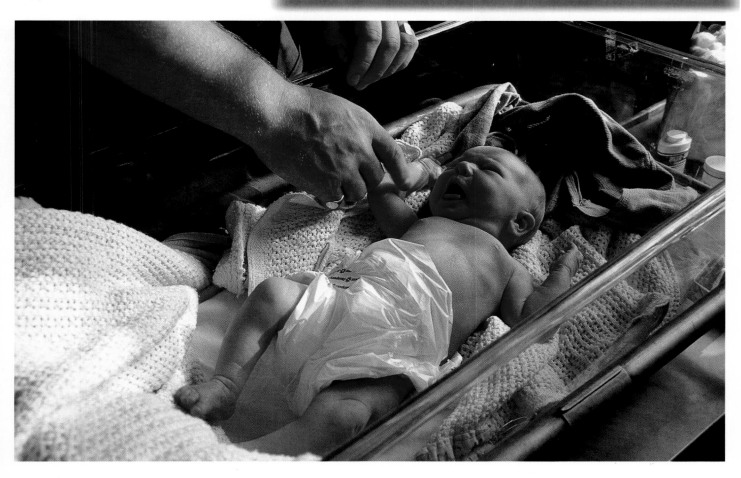

# The Christian Tradition

▲ *This nativity scene is in a cathedral in Trinidad. It shows the Holy Family, the infant Jesus with his parents, Mary and Joseph.*

The greatest birth celebration of all in the Christian church is the birth of Jesus Christ, which is celebrated on Christmas Day. Christians believe that Jesus was born 2,000 years ago in a stable in Bethlehem in the Holy Land. Today the celebration of his birth is one of the most important dates in the Christian calendar.

## Praying for a baby

The desire for children is mentioned several times in the Christian holy book, the Bible. During a wedding ceremony, producing children is listed as one of the reasons for marriage.

If they are having problems conceiving, some couples may go to the House of the Virgin Mary in Ephesus, an ancient Greek city, to pray for the much-wanted child. Mary was the mother of Jesus, and she is honored by Christians around the world.

▲ *Couples sometimes go to the house of the Virgin Mary to pray for a child. Mary, as the mother of Jesus, is believed to be able to help women who want to become parents.*

# A baby on the way

Although most babies are born healthy, sometimes they can have illnesses or disabilities. An expectant mother may wonder if the baby will be born safely. Toward the end of her pregnancy, she can ask her local priest to anoint her with holy oil as a prayer for a safe birth. The priest visits the mother-to-be at home or in the hospital, bringing oil that has been blessed, or consecrated. He uses the holy oil to make the sign of the cross (the symbol of Christianity) on her forehead. After a safe birth, the parents may go to church to give thanks to God.

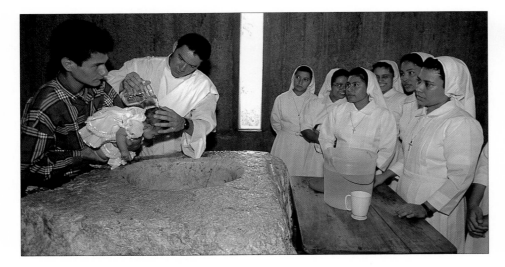

▲ *At this baptism ceremony in Nicaragua, the priest pours water over the child. Catholics believe that even young babies are born sinners, and the water removes these sins.*

# Baptism

Christian parents usually decide to have their baby baptized in the church as a way of welcoming it into Christianity. Baptism often takes place when the baby is a few months old. The parents can ask for a private baptism, with only invited guests present. These days, however, it is more common for a baby to be baptized as part of a church service, with the congregation joining in the celebration.

# Godparents

The parents often ask two close friends or relatives to be godparents. Godparents are friends or relatives who are given special responsibility for looking after the child if his or her parents cannot for some reason. Traditionally, they were expected to see that the child was brought up as a true Christian, but nowadays they are chosen to support and guide the child.

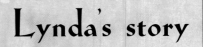

## Lynda's story

"My name is Lynda. I went to the christening of my baby brother, Mark. He was dressed in a long white lace dress that my grandmother, my mother, and then I had been christened in. I can't remember my christening—it was when I was a baby. When he had been christened, we all went in a procession to the front of the church. I carried a lighted candle to welcome my brother into the world. The priest held him up to show all the people. Then he gave him back to my mother."

# The service

A baptism or christening usually takes place at a morning service. The christening party stands around the font—a large vessel containing holy water. The rest of the congregation turns to face the font. During the baptism, parents and godparents promise that they will bring the child up in the Christian faith. The baby is named at this ceremony. The parents are asked to give the name they have chosen for the child (the Christian name). Often, the minister or priest pours a little holy water on the baby's forehead and makes the sign of the cross. The water symbolizes washing away sins and making a fresh start. The priest then calls the baby by name and welcomes him or her into the Christian Church.

The service is often followed by a party at the parents' house or in a restaurant, and friends and relatives bring gifts to the baby. Babies often receive lots of silver gifts. Silver objects are supposed to give a child a lucky start in life.

▼ Traditionally, parents choose two godparents for their child — often one of each sex. It is a real honor to be a godparent, because it means that the parents of your godchild place great trust in you to help in the upbringing of their baby.

# The Jewish Tradition

The holy book of Judaism is the *Torah*, or the Five Books of Moses. According to the teachings of the *Torah*, the most important ceremony for a baby boy is circumcision. The *Torah* says that a command was given by God to Abraham (the founder of the Jewish nation, who lived around 1400 B.C.) that "Every male among you who is eight days old must be circumcised."

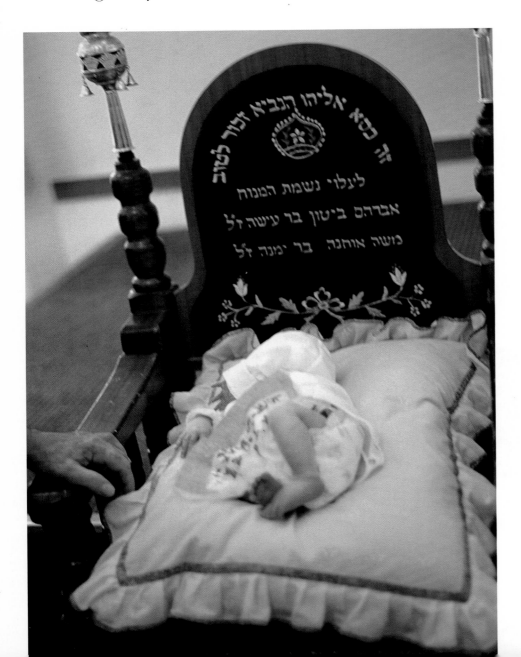

◀ This baby is lying on Elijah's chair. Elijah was a Hebrew prophet who lived about 800 B.C. He was said to have brought a woman's child back to life. Traditionally Jews believe that he protects and cares for children.

## Sacred text

9  And God said unto Abraham: "And as for thee, thou shalt keep My covenant, thou, and thy seed after thee throughout their generations.

10  This is My covenant, which ye shall keep between Me and you and thy seed after thee: every male among you shall be circumcised.

11  And ye shall be circumcised in the flesh of your foreskin; and it shall be a token of a covenant between Me and you.

12  And he that is eight days old shall be circumcised among you, every male throughout your generations...."

The Bible, Genesis 17

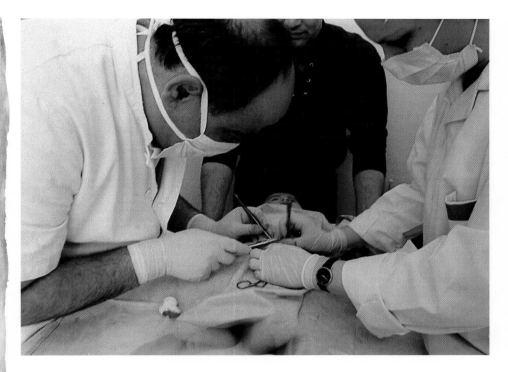

▲ *The circumcision ceremony marks the boy's official entrance into the Jewish community.*

# What is circumcision?

Circumcision is an operation during which the foreskin is removed from the penis. Circumcision forms part of the naming ceremony and marks the baby's entrance into the Jewish community and religion. This usually happens when the baby is eight days old.

There are some differences between the traditional (Orthodox Jewish) and the more modern (Conservative or Reform) ways of carrying out this ceremony. Often it takes place in the synagogue, the Jewish place of worship. In the United States and Europe, however, it is now more usual for the ceremony to take place at home or in the hospital. The actual circumcision is traditionally carried out by a specialist called a *mohel*, though it is sometimes performed by a doctor.

◀ *The circumcision of a baby boy is a time of great celebrations.*

# A traditional ceremony

Only men and boys attend a traditional circumcision ceremony in the synagogue. The men and boys who have celebrated their *Bar Mitzvah* or coming-of-age ceremony wear *kippahs* and prayer shawls. The baby is brought in by his godfather to be welcomed by the *rabbi*, the leader of the synagogue. The *rabbi* and the people at the ceremony welcome the baby by saying, "Blessed be he who enters." The godfather holds the baby boy while the *mohel* carries out the circumcision and the boy's father recites a blessing.

The ceremony ends with prayers for the baby's health and wishes for his future. Then the baby's names in Hebrew and English are announced, and everyone joins together to celebrate with a party.

## Rudi's story

"My name is Rudi. My brother had his naming ceremony at home when he was eight days old. The *mohel* told us about the Covenant where it says why circumcision is an important reminder of our promise to worship only God. Then he said a blessing while he did the circumcision. After the ceremony, we had a party to celebrate. As Jews, we believe that it is important to have children so that you can pass on your beliefs and ideas through the generations."

# Ceremonies today

Today, some Jewish communities have adapted this ceremony with the introduction of a naming ceremony for female babies. The words used are similar to those in the boy's circumcision ceremony, though there is no surgical operation. The baby girl is welcomed into the Jewish community as the people say, "Blessed is she who enters." Both parents announce her name in Hebrew and English, and recite a blessing. They speak of their wishes and hopes for her.

After these ceremonies, there is usually a special festive meal for family and guests.

▼ *Family and friends gather at a festive meal to celebrate the naming of a baby. They show their support for the baby and his or her parents by bringing gifts for the child and giving speeches.*

# The Muslim Tradition

Islam is more a way of life than a religion, because the whole of Islamic life is based on its rules. It originated in the Middle East but has now spread to almost every country in the world.

▼ *Prayer is a very important part of Muslim life. Children are taught how to recite prayers at an early age.*

## The first day of life

A new baby is seen as a gift from God by Muslims, so a birth is a time of great celebration. Several rituals are normally carried out soon afterward. These customs are intended to start the baby off on the path to becoming a true Muslim.

Muslims believe that the first thing a newborn baby should hear is the call to prayer, or *Adhan*, whispered in the right ear. The father or the *imam* (the person who leads prayers in the mosque) whispers these words: "Allah is the greatest. I bear witness that there is no god but Allah. I bear witness that Muhammad is the messenger of Allah. Hurry to prayer. Hurry to success. Allah is the greatest." The *Iqamah*, the call to stand for prayer, which is similar to the *Adhan*, is whispered into the baby's left ear.

# Circumcision

Muslim boys are often circumcised, usually when they are a few days old. However, some Muslims leave this until the boy is at least four years old. Muslims believe it is more hygienic for a boy to be circumcised. Circumcision is one of the most important rites of passage in a Muslim boy's life. It marks his entry into the Muslim faith.

## Sacred text

To God belongs the dominion
Of the heavens and the earth.
He creates what he wills
(And plans). He bestows
(Children) male or female
According to his Will (and Plan).

The *Koran*,
Sura XLII: 49

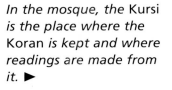

*In the mosque, the* Kursi *is the place where the* Koran *is kept and where readings are made from it.* ▶

◀ Muslim babies are often named after Muslim prophets who are mentioned in the Koran. Or they may be given names that reflect the name of Allah, such as Abdullah.

# The naming ceremony

When the baby is a few days old, most parents prepare for the *Aqiqah*, or naming ceremony. Friends and relatives are invited to the celebration, which can take place at the family home or in the mosque.

# Clean and pure

Muslims wash in a ritual before prayer so that they are clean and pure. So the baby is washed before the naming ceremony. This symbolizes the clean and fresh beginning of a new life. Some Muslims also shave a baby's head and weigh the hair. The parents will then make a gift to the poor, of the same weight as the baby's hair—gold for a boy and silver for a girl. A tiny baby does not often have much hair, so parents usually give more gold or silver than the agreed weight as a gesture of their joy at the birth.

## Imran's story

"My name is Imran. When our baby was a few days old, we gave her a taste of honey, just a little. It is a Muslim tradition that giving a new baby something sweet to taste so early in life makes him or her sweet-tempered. The baby was born in the hospital, so we did this ceremony when we got home, and said a prayer for her. We then had a big feast in a local restaurant with all our friends and family around us. It was a party to welcome our baby into the family and the way of Islam."

The *Adhan* and the *Iqamah* are said again at the ceremony, and the baby is given a taste of honey as a symbol of the sweetness of prayer. The baby's name will probably also have some religious significance. Boys are often named after one of the prophets of Islam, while girls may be given names of members of Muhammad's family. After the ceremony, there is a celebration feast. In Arab countries, if the baby is a boy, two goats are killed for the feast, and if it is a girl, one goat. Traditionally, one-third of the meat is given to the poor. Muslims believe that giving gifts is a way of thanking Allah for the baby.

▼ When Muslim women give birth, the Koran says that their husbands must tell family and friends of the birth and spread the news of the blessing that they have received from Allah.

# The Buddhist Tradition

▲ *The story of the birth of Buddha is told to children to make them aware of the importance of Buddha's teachings. Often Buddhists paint and draw images from the stories to illustrate the tale.*

## Sacred text

May all without exception be happy,
Beings seen or unseen,
Those who live near or far away,
Those who are born
And those who are not yet born.
May all beings be happy.

*Metta Sutta*
(Buddha's words on kindness)

Buddhism began in the Far East, but it is now one of the fastest-growing religions in the West. Buddhist traditions have spread throughout North America, Europe, and Australia, and Buddhist teachers from the Far East have moved to North America and Europe to teach the religion.

Buddhists in different parts of the world have different traditions and festivals, but they all celebrate the birth of the religion's founder, who came to be known as Buddha. This is probably the most important celebration in Buddhism. It is called *Wesak*, or *Vesac*, and it is celebrated on the day of the full moon in June or July. People visit temples and drape images of Buddha with flowers, incense, and candles to celebrate his birth. Some decorate their houses with lanterns and flowers, and there are processions through the streets.

Stories of Buddha's birth are told when a baby is born in the hope that he or she will then accept spiritual guidance from Buddhist teachers as they grow up. A traditional account of Buddha's birth says that one night, before he was born, his mother dreamed that a white elephant entered her womb. From this dream, priests predicted that her son would be a teacher who would influence the world. Many magical things are said to have happened as the baby Buddha was born.

# Birth in Buddhism

In Buddhism, birth is a time of hope and looking to the future. Buddhists believe that everybody should try to be kind and aware so that they can achieve freedom from suffering (*nirvana*) and help others to do the same.

▼ *At the* Wesak *celebration Buddhists listen to the teachings of Buddha and chant Buddhist texts.*

# Welcoming the baby

Buddhists believe that people should make up their own minds about whether to follow a religion and that a child should decide what to do when he or she is old enough to understand. However, a baby can still be brought up in the Buddhist way of life.

After the birth, monks may be invited to the family home to chant from the sacred (holy) texts and bless the baby. The monks wear long robes that are often orange, though different branches of Buddhists wear different colors.

▼ *This monk is chanting sacred texts to bless the young baby. The baby's older brother is joining in the prayers for his brother.*

▲ *Buddha was not a god, but Buddhists worship his images, such as these in Rangoon, Burma, and make offerings to them.*

# Joanne's story

"My name is Joanne. We invited monks to our house to bless my baby brother. They chanted verses from the scriptures. Chanting is an important part of Buddhist ceremonies in temples and monasteries, or at home, because it focuses the mind on what is happening. It is also important for me to learn to meditate. Meditation frees your mind from worries, so you can understand more about life."

# The naming ceremony

The naming ceremony takes place when the baby is about a month old. This may happen in the temple, and family and friends are invited. In the temple, parents and friends kneel and bow before a statue of Buddha and make offerings of flowers, candles, and incense. A monk may be asked to bless the child and name him or her. In some branches of Buddhism, sacred threads are tied around the baby's wrists to welcome *khwan*, a spirit that looks after babies.

# The Hindu Tradition

Hinduism began in India, which is where many Hindus still live. However, about one-third of Hindus now live in other parts of the world, particularly in North America, Australia, and Great Britain.

## Praying for the baby

Hindus place great importance on visiting the *mandir*, their temple or place of worship. Family life, which includes extended families and the Hindu community as a whole, is also very important. People believe that marriage is a partnership for producing children. When a woman is expecting a baby, family members go to the temple to pray for the child's future health and happiness.

While the mother is pregnant, she reads and recites from the Hindu scriptures, so that they will protect the baby and have a positive influence. The parents also make offerings of cooked rice to the god Vishnu to make the baby strong.

*By reading to the unborn baby in the womb, the mother is not only starting her child's religious life, she is also creating a feeling of closeness with her child.* ▶

Hindus believe that there are steps in a person's life that should be celebrated with special ceremonies. Offerings are made to the gods, and purification rituals take place. There are 16 of these steps, called *samskaras*—one to celebrate each stage of life. The first three *samskaras* take place before conception. Six take place between the child's birth and the sacred thread ritual—a ceremony for boys when they are older. This marks their rebirth as Hindus. Some of the early *samskaras* are the *Jatakarma*, which takes place after birth before the umbilical cord is severed, the *Namakarana*, the naming of the child, and the *Annaprasana*, the first time the baby is fed cooked rice.

▼ *This Hindu fortune teller tells horoscopes for a living. He predicts what the child will become when he or she is older, whether the child will make a good marriage, and how successful and happy he or she will be.*

When the baby is born, a priest visits the family to tell a horoscope. The horoscope shows the position of the stars and planets on the day of the baby's birth. From this, facts about the baby's future can be determined.

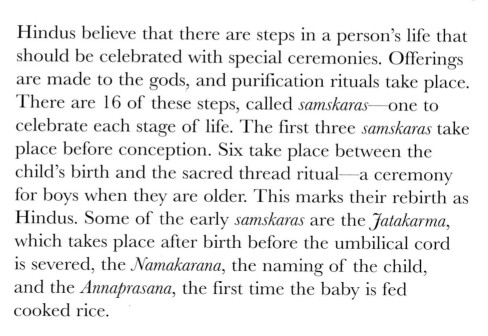

## Sacred text

I am he; you are she.
I am song; you are verse.
I am heaven; you are earth.
Let us two dwell together here; let us generate children.

*Atharva Veda* (the holiest book of knowledge): Marriage Mantra

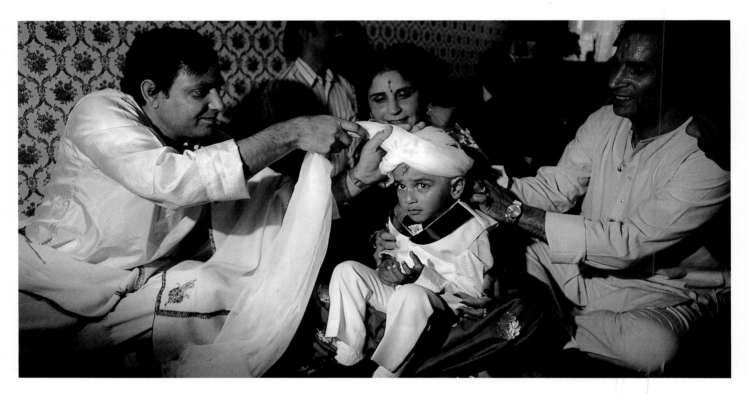

▲ *This young Hindu boy is about to have his head shaved to remove any evil from past lives.*

# Steps along the path of life

The first ceremony after the baby is born is when a special word, *AUM*, is written on his or her tongue with a pen dipped in honey. The word stands for the names of the three most important Hindu gods, which are different aspects of the Supreme Spirit, Brahman. In many families, there is a ceremony when the baby is ten days old. The baby's ears are pierced and hair is cut for the first time. In some families, this is left until the baby is a few months old. The baby is given a name at a ceremony conducted by the *pundit*, or holy man, in the *mandir*.

## Deva's story

"My name is Deva. When our baby was born, we wrote down the time and the day so that the priest could read a horoscope. It is important to choose the right name for a baby. The priest suggested which syllables should be included in the name. After the naming ceremony, we had a celebration when specially blessed food called *prasadam* was shared between us all."

The baby's first outing to see the sun is also a cause for celebration. He or she is dressed in new clothes and taken to the temple, or sometimes to the shrine of a local Mother Goddess. At five months old, the baby is given its first solid food at a ceremony, accompanied by prayers.

# A good start in life

When the baby is one year old, his or her head is shaved for the first time. Hindus believe that a person goes through many lives. When he or she dies, the soul is reborn into another body, which can be human or animal. Therefore, the baby has had many past lives, and shaving the head removes any evil from the past and gives the baby a good start. The child's head is shaved again at three and five years old.

▼ *When the child has its first haircut, the parents keep the hair to remember the landmark in the child's development.*

# The Sikh Tradition

Sikhism began in India and has now spread all over the world. The founder of the religion was Guru Nanak, who was born in 1469. The date of his birth and the birth of the other *gurus* (leaders) is a cause for celebration among Sikhs. These celebrations, or *Gurpurbs,* are usually marked at the Sikh place of worship, the *gurdwara,* with *akand path* (continuous reading of the holy text, the *Guru Granth Sahib*). There is also *kirtan* (playing hymns from the *Guru Granth Sahib*) as well as *katha* (Sikh stories and verses). Some places also have *nagar kirtan,* where there is a procession with the *Guru Granth Sahib* headed by five Sikhs carrying *nishan sahibs* (the Sikh flag). Sweets are also offered to the people outside the temple.

▲ *Sikhs in England parade through the streets. They carry the Sikh flag to celebrate the birthday of Guru Nanak.*

# Welcoming the baby

▼ A father and son stand outside the Golden Temple at Amritsar, the holiest place for Sikhs. The father will coach his son in the Sikh way of worship throughout life.

It is very important to Sikh families that their children are brought up as Sikhs and understand the Sikh beliefs and way of life. When a baby is born, the father tells the family's friends and relatives and gives presents of sweets to neighbors and friends. Sometimes a respected member of the community visits the house and gives the baby a few drops of honey and water while reciting the first five verses of the *Japji*. This is a hymn written by Guru Nanak, the first and one of the most respected Sikh *gurus*. When the mother and baby are well enough, the family and guests go to the *gurdwara* for the naming ceremony.

## Sacred text

God has been kind to me. The almighty one has fulfilled my longing. I have come home purified by God's love and obtained blessings, happiness, and peace. O saintly people, only God's Name can give us true liberty. Always remember God and keep doing good, day and night.

Sikh hymn used at the naming ceremony

▲ *At this naming ceremony the mother and baby are given amrit (sweet water).*

# The naming ceremony

At the *gurdwara*, the parents recite hymns from the *Guru Granth Sahib* to celebrate the birth of the new child. *Karah prashad* (sacred pudding) is prepared by the family. *Amrit* (sweet water) is also prepared and given to the baby and the mother. The parents bring new *rumalas*, cloths for covering the *Guru Granth Sahib*, to the naming ceremony.

## Hardeep's story

"My name is Hardeep. There are often naming ceremonies at the *gurdwara* I go to. The *granthi* sometimes gives the baby a *kara*, a steel bracelet. It is a complete circle that shows that there is one God and one truth without beginning or end. The steel of the bracelet means strength. The *kara* is one of the Five Ks that Sikh men should wear: uncut hair (*kesh*); sword (*kirpan*); underwear (*katcha*); comb (*kanga*); and bracelet (*kara*)."

There are hymns giving thanks for the new baby, and the parents' names are mentioned during the *Ardas*, a prayer that is said by everyone. There are no priests in Sikhism, so readers, called *granthi*, read from the *Guru Granth Sahib*. Any member of the congregation can speak at a service. The *Guru Granth Sahib* is placed on a platform behind a canopy, and the reader sits behind facing the people.

After the prayer there is a reading from the *Guru Granth Sahib*. This is not planned but is picked at random. The baby's parents then choose a name that begins with the first letter of the reading. The name is followed by *Singh* ("lion") for a boy or *Kaur* ("princess") for a girl. The *granthi* usually gives a baby boy his first steel bracelet, or *kara*, at the naming ceremony.

*The* granthi *reads from the* Guru Granth Sahib. *Like all Sikh men, he wears a turban, because one of the five special signs of being a Sikh is to have uncut hair.* ▼

# GLOSSARY

**Allah** (AWL-uh) the Muslim God.

**Buddha** (BOOD-uh) Siddhartha Gautama, an Indian prince who founded Buddhism.

**conception** (con-SEP-shun) when a male sperm fertilizes a female egg.

**congregation** (con-gruh-GAY-shun) a gathering of people for worship.

**covenant** (CUV-uh-nent) an agreement entered into between God and a person or people.

**granthi** (GRAN-tee) a Sikh priest.

**gurdwara** (GOOR-dwa-ruh) a Sikh place of worship.

**guru** (GOO-roo) a Sikh leader.

**Guru Granth Sahib** (GOO-roo GRANT SAW-eeb) the Sikh holy book.

**image** (IM-uj) a statue or likeness of something or someone.

**incense** (IN-cents) a scented stick that is burned to give a fragrant smell.

**kara** (KAW-ruh) a bracelet worn by Sikh men and women.

**kirpan** (KUR-pun) a dagger carried by Sikh men and women.

**Koran** (coh-RAN) the Muslim holy book.

**Langar** (lan-GHAR) the Sikh tradition of a shared kitchen, where all visitors and Sikhs can share a meal together.

**mandir** (MAN-deer) a Hindu temple.

**meditation** (med-uh-TAY-shun) to exercise the mind by focusing on just one idea. Meditation is said to lead to nirvana (perfect bliss) because it teaches wisdom and calms one down.

**mohel** (MOW-ell) a Jew who performs a circumcision.

**monastery** (MON-uh-stair-ee) a place where monks live and worship.

**mosque** (MOSK) a Muslim place of worship.

**nirvana** (nur-VAHN-uh) the state of blissful calmness achieved by Buddha, that all Buddhists try to reach.

**prophet** (PROF-ut) someone who foretells things about a religion.

**rabbi** (RAB-eye) a leader of the Jewish religion.

**ritual** (RIT-you-ell) an action or custom that forms part of a ceremony.

**sacred** (SAY-kred) something that is holy.

**scriptures** (SKRIP-toors) holy writings.

**symbolize** (SIM-buh-lies) to represent something.

**synagogue** (SIN-uh-gog) a Jewish place of worship.

**Torah** (TOR-uh) the holy book of the Jews.

# FURTHER INFORMATION

## Books

Chambers, Catherine. *Sikh* (Beliefs and Cultures). Danbury, CT: Children's Press, 1997.

Ganeri, Anita. *Buddhist* (Beliefs and Cultures). Danbury, CT: Children's Press, 1997.

Goldman, Alex J. *I Am a Holocaust Torah*. Hewlett, NY: Gefen, 2000.

Hunter, Elrose. *The Story Atlas of the Bible*. Parsippany, NJ: Silver Burdett Press, 1996.

Kenley, Karyn. *My Favorite Bible Stories* (The Beginner's Bible). New York: Little Moorings, 1995.

Penney, Sue. *Judaism*. Austin, TX: Raintree Steck-Vaughn, 1997.

————. *Sikhism*. Austin, TX: Raintree Steck-Vaughn, 1997.

Quinn, Daniel P. *I Am Buddhist*. New York: Rosen Group, 1996.

Rock, Lois. *The Time of Jesus*. Colorado Springs, CO: Lion Children's Books, 1999.

Wood, Angela. *Buddhist Temple*. Milwaukee, WI: Gareth Stevens, 2000.

————. *Hindu Mandir*. Milwaukee, WI: Gareth Stevens, 2000.

GENERAL SERIES ON RELIGION:

Beliefs and Cultures series (Children's Press, 1996–1997)

Discovering Religions series (Raintree Steck-Vaughn, 1997.)

## Websites

http://www.sikhfoundation.org/ – The Sikh Foundation

http://www.hindusamajtemple.org/ht/hindu.html – An introduction to Hinduism

http://www.islamicity.org/ – An introduction to the world of Islam

http://conline.net/ – Christians Online, a Christian resource

http://www.jewishweb.com/ – The worldwide Jewish Web

# INDEX

All the numbers in **bold** refer to photographs.